SEEING TWO WORLDS

A Journey Through Autism and Schizophrenia

Travis Breeding

Travis Breeding

CONTENTS

INTRODUCTION

My name is Travis, and I am a person living with schizophrenia. I first experienced the symptoms of this mental illness at the age of 28 and was diagnosed by a psychiatrist. Before then, I was diagnosed with Asperger Syndrome at the age of 22. This book is about my journey with schizophrenia and how I have managed the disorder over the years.

My experience with schizophrenia has been one of fear and confusion. I experience hallucinations, which tell me to cut body parts out of myself. I also have delusions, which are fixed false beliefs that I persistently hold onto despite evidence to the contrary. My delusions take many different forms, from believing that I have supernatural powers to believing that I am constantly being watched.

I have tried many different treatments over the years in order to manage my symptoms. I have worked closely with a psychiatrist and have used antipsychotic drugs to control my symptoms. I have also used mindfulness and cognitive behavior therapy to help me gain control of my mind.

This book will provide readers with a better understanding of what it is like to live with schizophrenia. It will also provide insight into my experience with the different treatments I have tried, and the effects they have had on my mental health. I will talk about the obstacles I have faced, along with the successes and failures. I will also provide five examples of delusional thoughts that I have had over the years.

The delusional thoughts I have experienced over the years include believing that I have supernatural powers, like being able to read people's minds. I have also believed that I am constantly being watched, that I have a disease which will soon cause me to die, and that I have special connections with certain celebrities. I have also struggled with believing that I am receiving special messages from the government, and that I have been chosen to lead an important mission.

Through this book, I hope to provide readers with a better understanding of what it is like to live with schizophrenia. I also want to provide insight into the different treatments I have tried over the years and the effects they have had on my mental health. I hope that this book will raise awareness about this mental illness and will help to reduce the stigma surrounding it.

CHAPTER 1 AUTISM DIAGNOSIS

I'm 20 years old, at college, but something's wrong. I can't figure it out. I'm too tired and too anxious and too scared to really think about it, so I just try to keep my head down and my eyes to the ground, hoping that if I can just get through the day I'll find some clarity.

But the dread and confusion never go away. Everywhere I go I feel like I'm under a microscope, like I'm being judged and found wanting. It's like I'm walking through mud, dragging myself from one class to the next and feeling like I'm never going to make it.

I know something isn't right, but I don't know what it is. I've been to the campus clinic, and they couldn't tell me anything. I've tried talking to my friends and family, but they just say my problems are normal. I'm starting to think that maybe I'm going crazy and no one can help me.

I decide to visit a therapist near campus. The first visit is a little awkward, but she listens and asks thoughtful questions. We talk about my feelings of loneliness and confusion, and she decides to do some tests to see if she can get to the root of the problem.

I take a battery of tests, and it's not until I'm finished that

I realize how nervous I've been. The therapist studies the results for a few minutes and then looks me in the eye. "Robert," she says, "I have a diagnosis for you."

My heart sinks, knowing I'm about to receive a label that I'll have to live with for the rest of my life. She tells me I have Asperger Syndrome, Bipolar Disorder, and Obsessive Compulsive Disorder.

I'm 22, and I'm stunned. It's like the world has suddenly stopped spinning. How could this be happening? I thought I was just going through the normal stresses of college life, but now I'm facing something much more serious.

In that moment, I decided that I'm going to take control of my future. I know that I'm going to need a lot of help, but I also know that I'm the only person who can take the first steps.

So I did. I made an appointment with a doctor to get a comprehensive physical and mental health assessment. I talked to my family about my diagnosis, and I started researching the different treatments available. I joined a support group for people with mental health issues and started seeing a mental health counselor. I started taking medications to help manage my symptoms.

I also started exercising more, eating healthier, and taking up yoga and meditation. I began to take more classes that interested me, and eventually changed my major to something that felt more meaningful. I reached out to people I hadn't talked to in a while, and I started to slowly rebuild my life.

It's been fifteen years since I was diagnosed, and a lot has changed. I still have bad days, but I'm more aware of my triggers and I have more tools to manage my symptoms. It's been a long journey, and I still have a lot of work to do, but I'm getting better every day.

My life is not what I thought it would be, but I'm learning to accept it. I'm learning that there's strength in accepting my diagnosis, and the journey has given me a new appreciation for the beauty in life. Now, I'm pushing through the darkness, no matter how deep it gets.

CHAPTER 2 SEEKING INFORMATION

I had been living with Asperger Syndrome for most of my life, but it was only during my early thirties that I became aware of this and started to look for ways to manage the difficulties I often experienced due to the condition. This led me to discover the works of Tony Attwood and his books on Asperger Syndrome, which I began to read voraciously.

At first, I wasn't sure if I should believe what Attwood was saying or if his books would even be helpful to me. But as I continued to read, I found that his research and insights were so insightful and full of empathy that I couldn't help but be drawn in. His words gave me the courage to accept my diagnosis and to look for real, practical ways to improve my quality of life.

To do this, I began to focus on studying social skills and understanding how I could use them to cope with some of the difficulties I faced on a daily basis. I started by reading Attwood's books, including his seminal work, "Asperger Syndrome: A Guide for Parents and Professionals". This book provided a wealth of information about Asperger Syndrome, including the various traits and characteristics which can manifest in people with the condition.

It was through Attwood's book that I was able to gain an understanding of the difficulties I was facing, and how they might be related to my condition. Attwood's book also provided me with a deeper level of insight into the importance of learning social skills and building relationships. This was something I had struggled with for many years, and Attwood's book provided me with the information and understanding I needed to start making progress.

One of the key strategies I learned from Attwood's books was the importance of being aware of one's own needs and feelings. This was something I had struggled with for many years, as I often found myself overwhelmed with emotions and unable to process them. Attwood's books provided me with the tools and strategies I needed to start understanding myself better, and to better regulate my emotions.

Another key strategy I learned from Attwood's books was the importance of developing meaningful relationships with other people. This was something I had often found difficult due to my difficulty understanding social cues and my tendency to become overwhelmed by others. Attwood's books helped me to understand the importance of being present in social situations and actively engaging with others, as well as being aware of the impact my behaviour can have on those around me.

I also learned from Attwood's books the importance of taking regular breaks from social situations and activities. This was something I had often struggled with, as I found it difficult to stay focused in social situations. Attwood's books provided me with strategies to manage my energy levels and to understand when it was appropriate to take a break.

Furthermore, Attwood's books also helped me to gain an understanding of the importance of self-care and self-compassion. This was something I had often struggled with, as I had difficulty managing my emotions and was often judgemental towards myself. Attwood's books provided me with the strategies I needed to start being kinder to myself and to cultivate a more compassionate attitude towards myself and my condition.

In addition, Attwood's books provided me with strategies to better manage my stress levels. This was something I had often struggled with, as I found it difficult to manage my emotions and my energy levels. Attwood's books provided me with strategies to become more aware of my own stress levels and to be able to better regulate them.

Finally, Attwood's books helped me to gain an understanding of the importance of setting boundaries and learning to say no. This was something I had often struggled with, as I found it difficult to assert myself in social situations. Attwood's books provided me with the tools and strategies I needed to start setting boundaries and understanding the importance of saying no when necessary.

These are just a few of the key strategies I learned from Tony Attwood's books on Asperger Syndrome. His books provided me with the information and understanding I needed to start making progress in managing my condition and improving my quality of life. His words gave me the courage and strength I needed to accept my diagnosis, and to find practical ways to manage the difficulties I faced on a daily basis.

CHAPTER 3 TRYING TO MAKE FRIENDS

Making Friends When You're on the Autism Spectrum

Making friends is an important part of life, especially for those on the autism spectrum. Unfortunately, those on the autism spectrum can often have difficulty connecting with others. This can be due to a range of factors, such as difficulty understanding social cues, difficulty communicating, and difficulty connecting with others on an emotional level. Despite these challenges, there are a number of strategies and tips that autistic people can use to make friends.

1. Accept Yourself- The first and most important step in making friends when you're on the autism spectrum is to accept and embrace your own unique qualities. Accepting yourself is the key to forming meaningful relationships with others. It's important to remember that everyone is unique, including those on the autism spectrum. By accepting and embracing your unique qualities and strengths, you'll be better equipped to connect with others in meaningful ways.

2. Educate Yourself- Learning more about autism is a great way to gain a better understanding of yourself, as well as how to interact with others. Doing research on autism,

attending seminars and workshops, and connecting with other individuals on the autism spectrum can help you become more confident in making connections with new people.

3. Think About What You Have to Offer- It's important to remember that everyone has something to offer in relationships. Think about the skills, interests, and qualities that you have to offer and use them to your advantage when meeting new people.

4. Join a Special Interest Group- Joining a special interest group that caters to individuals on the autism spectrum can be a great way to make friends and connect with others. Look for a group in your area that has activities and events that you enjoy.

5. Be Open-Minded and Curious- Being open-minded and curious is key when it comes to making friends. Ask questions, and be willing to try new things and meet new people. You never know who you might meet and what connections you might make.

6. Find Common Ground- One of the best ways to make friends is to look for common ground. This could include shared interests, hobbies, beliefs, or values. This can be a great way to find people who share similar passions or who might be interested in the same things as you.

7. Take the Initiative- Don't be afraid to take the initiative when it comes to making friends. Reach out to someone who you think you might get along with, and introduce yourself. A great way to do this is by sending a message on a social media platform, or going up to someone in your area to introduce yourself.

8. Show Interest- Showing interest in someone is a great way to start forming a connection. When someone talks about something that interests them, ask follow-up questions and show genuine interest in what they are saying. This will show them that you are interested in getting to know them and help form a connection.

9. Show Respect- It's important to show respect to those around you, especially when it comes to making friends. Respect other people's boundaries and opinions, and be polite and courteous in all interactions. Respect is a key ingredient in any friendship.

10. Practice Social Skills- As someone on the autism spectrum, it's important to practice social skills in order to make friends. This can include things like learning how to make small talk, how to read body language, and how to start and maintain conversations.

11. Express Yourself- Being able to express yourself authentically and openly is important in any relationship. Don't be afraid to be yourself and share your thoughts and feelings with others. Expressing yourself honestly can help form strong friendships.

12. Hang Out with People- In order to make friends, it's important to spend time with people. Try to hang out with people as often as you can. This could include going to events, social gatherings, or just meeting up with someone for coffee.

13. Make Eye Contact- Eye contact is an important part of any social interaction. When talking to someone, make sure to look them in the eye and maintain eye contact. This will show that you are engaged in the conversation and

interested in getting to know the person.

14. Be Positive- Staying positive when making friends is essential. It's important to be encouraging, supportive, and uplifting when interacting with others. People are more likely to gravitate towards those who are positive and have a good outlook on life.

15. Participate in Activities- Participating in activities is a great way to make friends. Look for activities in your area that you enjoy and try to attend them as often as possible. These activities can be anything from sports teams to volunteer organizations.

16. Be a Good Listener- Listening is an important part of any relationship. When talking to someone, practice being an active listener and make sure to give them your full attention. This will show that you are interested in getting to know them.

17. Ask for Help- Don't be afraid to ask for help when it comes to making friends. Ask your friends, family, or even professionals for advice and tips on how to make connections with others.

18. Take Things Slow- Relationships take time to develop, so be sure to take things slow when making friends. Don't expect to be best friends with someone right away. Allow time for the relationship to develop and grow.

19. Be patient- Patience is key when it comes to making friends. Not every interaction will be a success, and it can take time to find the right people who you click with. Don't give up and practice being patient.

20. Be Open to New Experiences- Being open to new

experiences is an important step in making friends. Try new activities and don't be afraid to step out of your comfort zone. This can help you meet new people and have a variety of experiences.

21. Offer to Help- Offering to help someone can be a great way to start making friends. You could offer to help with a project, lend a hand at an event, or just help out a friend in need. This will show that you care and are willing to be there for others.

22. Take an Interest in Others- Showing an interest in others is a great way to bond and build relationships. Ask questions and really get to know the people around you. Taking an interest in others will show them that you care and want to get to know them better.

23. Keep in Touch- It's important to stay in touch with the people you meet. Make sure to follow up with people after you meet them and stay in touch with those you meet in the future. This will show that you are interested in staying connected and forming deeper relationships.

24. Be Flexible- Being flexible is essential when making friends. Be willing to compromise, adapt, and adjust to different situations and make time for those you meet. This will show them that you are willing to work together to make the relationship work.

25. Have Fun- Above all else, have fun when making friends. Enjoy the process and don't take it too seriously. Spend time with people you enjoy and make sure to laugh and have a good time.

Once you've mastered the art of making friends, it's important to know how to keep them. Here are ten strategies that can help you maintain and strengthen friendships:

1. Show Appreciation- Showing appreciation and gratitude is a great way to show those in your life that you care. This could include sending a thank you card, leaving a positive review, or just saying thank you.

2. Make Time- Making time for friends is important. Try to schedule regular check-ins and hangouts as often as possible. This will show that you value your time with them and are making an effort to stay connected.

3. Be Honest- Honesty is essential in any relationship. Be honest and open with your friends and let them know when you're struggling or need help. This will show that you trust them and are willing to be vulnerable with them.

4. Support and Encourage- Show your friends that you're there for them by offering support and encouragement. Be there for them in times of need and celebrate their successes. This will show that you truly care and want to see them succeed.

5. Respect Boundaries- Respect your friends' boundaries and privacy. Don't pry into their personal lives or ask too many questions. This will show them that you respect their wishes and want to maintain a healthy and trusting relationship.

6. Listen- Listening is an important part of any friendship. Show your friends that you're there for them by being a good listener. Listen to their problems, offer advice, and be there for them when they need it.

7. Be Positive- A positive attitude can go a long way. Make

sure to stay positive and uplifting when interacting with friends. This will show them that you are supportive and care about their wellbeing.

8. Resolve Conflicts Quickly- Conflict is inevitable in relationships, but it's important to resolve conflicts quickly. Talk openly and honestly with your friends and work on resolving any issues. This will show them that you're willing to work together to maintain a strong relationship.

9. Compromise- Compromise is essential in any relationship. Be willing to compromise and adjust in order to maintain and strengthen your friendship.

10. Be Yourself- Above all else, it's important to be yourself. Don't be afraid to show your true self to your friends and let them get to know who you really are. This will show that you trust them and will help strengthen your relationship.

Making friends when you're on the autism spectrum can be challenging, but it doesn't have to be. By following the strategies outlined above, you can make meaningful connections and build strong and lasting friendships.

CHAPTER 4 A PSYCHOTIC BREAK

It was an ordinary day in early June when my first psychotic break occurred. I was 28 years old and had been feeling unusually anxious and depressed for several weeks. The anxiety and depression had become so debilitating that my relationship with my partner had begun to suffer, and I was struggling to maintain my job.

It was on that fateful day that my delusions began. I became convinced that I had cancer, and that the only way to save myself was to cut the cancer out of me and remove my thyroid.

I remember the fear that I felt as I considered the possibility of being diagnosed with such a serious illness. I felt as though I were in a nightmare, and that I was completely at the mercy of my delusions. I was desperate to make sense of what was happening to me and felt so confused and scared.

The experience of being inpatient at the hospital was a negative one. I felt as though I was being treated as though I were crazy, and I had no control over my own life. I was unable to make decisions for myself and had to rely on the opinions of the professionals around me. I felt as though I were a stranger in my own body, disconnected from the world around me and unable to make sense of what was happening.

As I gradually began to understand my condition, I started to realize that my experience was not uncommon. I began to read more about psychosis and learnt about the signs and symptoms that I had been experiencing. I also found comfort in the stories of others who had experienced similar episodes, which helped me to understand that I was not alone.

Although the experience was a difficult and frightening one, it ultimately led me to a better understanding of myself and my condition. I learnt to accept the reality of my psychosis and found ways to cope with my symptoms.

However, it is important to note that psychosis is a highly individual experience. What works for one person may not work for another, and it is important to be aware of the signs and symptoms of psychosis in order to identify and manage it in its early stages.

In this chapter, we will explore 20 key strategies that an individual can use to help determine if what they are experiencing is real or not.

1. Recognize and accept the reality of your experience. Acknowledge that your thoughts, feelings, and behaviors may not reflect reality and that you are not responsible for them.

2. Educate yourself about the signs and symptoms of psychosis. Knowing what to look for can help you be mindful of any changes in your behavior and help you identify when you may need extra support.

3. Speak to your healthcare provider about your experience. Your healthcare provider will be able to provide you with the necessary tools and resources to help manage your symptoms.

4. Connect with support networks. Reach out to family and friends who can provide emotional and practical support. Additionally, look into local support groups and activities that can help you connect with others who have had similar experiences.

5. Practice self-care. Taking care of yourself is an important part of managing your symptoms. Make sure you get enough rest and practice relaxation techniques such as yoga and meditation.

6. Make sure to eat healthy and exercise regularly. Eating a balanced diet and engaging in regular physical activity can help improve your overall wellbeing.

7. Pay attention to your triggers. Become aware of any situations or events that might trigger a psychotic episode and practice strategies to reduce your stress levels, such as deep breathing and mindfulness.

8. Practice grounding techniques. Grounding techniques are helpful for bringing yourself back to the present moment and calming your mind. Examples include focusing on your five senses, repeating a phrase, and focusing on a physical sensation.

9. Manage your stress levels. Finding ways to manage your stress levels, such as taking regular breaks and engaging in activities that you enjoy, can help reduce the intensity of psychotic episodes.

10. Make use of distraction techniques. Distraction techniques can be helpful in redirecting your attention away from unhelpful thoughts and feelings. Examples include reading a book, playing a game, or talking to a friend.

11. Practice cognitive behavioral therapy (CBT). CBT is a type of psychotherapy that can help you manage your thoughts and behaviors. It can help you recognize unhelpful thought patterns and replace them with more helpful ones.

12. Make sure to keep a healthy sleep schedule. Getting enough sleep is important for maintaining good mental health. Make sure to get plenty of rest and practice good sleep hygiene habits.

13. Minimize the use of drugs and alcohol. Substance abuse can worsen the symptoms of psychosis and should be avoided.

14. Take medication as prescribed. If you are prescribed medication, make sure to take it as prescribed by your doctor and never stop taking it without consulting your doctor first.

15. Seek professional help if needed. If your symptoms become unmanageable, reach out to your healthcare provider or a mental health professional for help.

16. Stay connected to your support network. Make sure to stay in touch with family, friends, and other support networks to stay connected and receive emotional support.

17. Practice self-compassion. Remind yourself that you are not alone and that you are doing the best you can.

18. Make time for yourself. Make sure to make time for activities that you enjoy and that bring you joy.

19. Set realistic goals. Break down tasks into smaller, achievable steps and take time to reward yourself for achieving each one.

20. Remain hopeful. Remember that there is a light at the end of the tunnel and that recovery is possible.

By following these strategies, you can help yourself move forward and make progress toward managing your psychosis. It is important to remember that recovery is possible and that with the right support, you can move forward with your life.

CHAPTER 5 WHAT IS WHAT?

Autism Spectrum Disorder (ASD) and Schizophrenia are two distinct neurological disorders with a few similarities and a great many differences. In this chapter, we will discuss how the two can be confused and misdiagnosed, explore the similarities and differences between the two disorders, and offer insight into how a person with autism may feel when they experience a period of delusional thinking. We will also compare and contrast 25 individual traits of autism and schizophrenia to further illustrate the distinctions between the two disorders.

One of the primary similarities between autism and schizophrenia is the fact that both disorders can lead to social withdrawal. People with autism may choose to isolate themselves because they find it difficult to understand or relate to others, and people with schizophrenia may distance themselves from social settings due to paranoia, fear of judgement, and confusion.

Misdiagnosis is a common problem between the two disorders. People with autism may be misdiagnosed with schizophrenia, and people with schizophrenia may be misdiagnosed with autism. One of the major causes of misdiagnosis is that some of the symptoms of one disorder may overlap with the symptoms of the other. For example, people with autism can appear socially disconnected and may have difficulty interacting with others, while people with schizophrenia can also exhibit signs of social withdrawal.

Another similarity between the two disorders is that both can manifest in different intensities. Autism is a spectrum disorder, meaning that symptoms can range from mild to severe. Likewise, schizophrenia can also range from mild to severe, depending on the individual's level of functioning.

Despite the similarities outlined above, there are many differences between autism and schizophrenia. One of the most significant differences is that people with schizophrenia experience psychosis, which is a break from reality that can include delusions and/or hallucinations. People with autism do not experience psychosis, but can sometimes experience a period of delusional thinking in which they create a make-believe world to cope with their autism. This can be confusing and can sometimes be mistaken for psychosis, but it is not the same.

The neurological differences between autism and schizophrenia are also significant. Autism is caused by biological differences in the brain related to communication, social interaction, and behavior regulation. Schizophrenia is caused by a combination of environmental and genetic factors that impact the brain's chemistry, leading to psychotic symptoms.

When it comes to treatment, the two disorders also have different approaches. People with autism may benefit from behavior modification and behavior therapy, while people with schizophrenia often require medications such as antipsychotics to control their symptoms.

To better illustrate the distinctions between autism and schizophrenia, let's compare and contrast the following 25 individual traits of each disorder:

1. Autistic people often prefer to be left alone and can appear socially disconnected. Schizophrenic people may also appear socially disconnected, but tend to feel paranoid in social situations and isolate themselves due to fear of judgement.

2. Autistic people often have difficulty initiating and maintaining conversations, as well as understanding social cues and expectations. Schizophrenic people may also struggle with these things, but are more likely to experience an inability to process their own thoughts and communicate them in a logical way.

3. Autistic people may have difficulty with sensory processing, such as getting overstimulated in loud or busy places. Schizophrenic people can also struggle with sensory processing, but may also experience visual, auditory, or tactile hallucinations.

4. Autistic people may display repetitive behaviors, such as hand-flapping or rocking. Schizophrenic people may also display unusual behaviors, such as talking to themselves or becoming preoccupied with a specific topic or idea.

5. Autistic people may have difficulty with social situations, but are unlikely to experience paranoia or delusional thoughts. Schizophrenic people may experience paranoia and delusions, as well as difficulty processing reality.

6. Autistic people may struggle with organization and executive functioning. Schizophrenic people may also struggle with organization, but may also have difficulty understanding cause and effect.

7. Autistic people may display unusual interests, such as a fascination with a particular topic or activity. Schizophrenic people may also focus on certain topics or activities, but they may be related to their delusions or hallucinations.

8. Autistic people may exhibit difficulty with maintaining eye contact. Schizophrenic people may also struggle with eye contact, but can also experience involuntary movements or change in their facial expressions.

9. Autistic people may display an inability to understand or interpret nonverbal cues, such as facial expressions or body language. Schizophrenic people may have difficulty understanding nonverbal cues as well, but may also have difficulty understanding the meaning or purpose of simple language.

10. Autistic people may have difficulty regulating their emotions and may become overwhelmed in certain situations. Schizophrenic people may also struggle with emotional regulation, but may have difficulty recognizing their own emotions and the emotions of others.

11. Autistic people may experience problems with sleep or have difficulty falling asleep. Schizophrenic people may also experience sleep disturbances, but they may also experience nightmares related to their delusions or hallucinations.

12. Autistic people may struggle with change and may become overwhelmed when faced with new situations. Schizophrenic people may also struggle with change, but may also become anxious or paranoid when faced with new stimuli.

13. Autistic people may become fixated on certain objects or activities and may prefer routine. Schizophrenic people may also become fixated on certain objects or activities, but they may become preoccupied with certain topics related to their delusions or hallucinations.

14. Autistic people may have difficulty understanding abstract concepts. Schizophrenic people may also struggle with abstract concepts, but may also experience difficulty comprehending simple language.

15. Autistic people may display difficulty with motor skills, such as handwriting or coordination. Schizophrenic people may also experience difficulty with motor skills, but may also experience difficulty with coordination due to tremors or other physical symptoms.

16. Autistic people may experience difficulty with making and sustaining relationships. Schizophrenic people may have difficulty with relationships as well, but may also become preoccupied with certain individuals because of their delusions or hallucinations.

17. Autistic people may be more sensitive to certain stimuli, such as light or sound. Schizophrenic people may also be sensitive to certain stimuli, but may also experience auditory or visual hallucinations.

18. Autistic people may become overwhelmed in

certain social situations, such as large groups or loud environments. Schizophrenic people may also become overwhelmed in certain social situations, but may also become anxious or paranoid due to their delusions or hallucinations.

19. Autistic people may be less likely to communicate with others, while schizophrenic people may communicate in an unusual or disorganized manner.

20. Autistic people may have difficulty understanding what someone is saying to them, while schizophrenic people may understand the words but not the meaning.

21. Autistic people may have difficulty with concentration, while schizophrenic people may become preoccupied with certain topics or ideas related to their delusions or hallucinations.

22. Autistic people may have difficulty with reading comprehension or understanding written language, while schizophrenic people may have difficulty understanding written language because of their delusions or hallucinations.

23. Autistic people may have difficulty with memory, while schizophrenic people may have difficulty forming, retaining, and retrieving memories due to their delusions or hallucinations.

24. Autistic people may struggle with transitions, while schizophrenic people may struggle with transitions because of their delusions or hallucinations.

25. Autistic people may experience difficulty with problem-solving, while schizophrenic people may struggle with

certain tasks because of their delusions or hallucinations.

As this chapter has illustrated, autism and schizophrenia are two distinct disorders, though they do share some similarities. People with autism may experience a period of delusional thinking in which they create a make-believe world to cope with their autism, but this should not be mistaken for psychosis. People with schizophrenia experience hallucinations and/or delusions and require medications to control their symptoms, whereas people with autism may benefit from behavior modification and behavior therapy. By comparing and contrasting the individual traits of autism and schizophrenia, we have gained a better understanding of the distinctions between the two disorders.

CHAPTER 6 FINDING AN IDENTITY

For years I have struggled with finding an identity that incorporates both my autism and schizophrenia diagnoses. As a person with a dual diagnosis, sometimes it is difficult for me to tell whether certain traits are attributed to autism or schizophrenia. I often feel like I am a walking contradiction. I am both autistic and schizophrenic and must figure out how I want to identify myself.

My autism diagnosis has been with me since I was a child. I remember being in the second grade and having my teachers call my parents to tell them I had difficulties paying attention in class. When I was eight, I was formally diagnosed with autism after a lengthy evaluation process. My autism diagnosis has allowed me to understand why I have difficulty conversing with people, why I often have difficulty understanding social cues, and why I often have difficulty paying attention in class.

I identify strongly with my autistic traits. I embrace the fact that I have difficulty understanding social rules and prefer to be alone and in my own little world. I have come to terms with the fact that I often need to take time to process things and that I have difficulty understanding the subtleties of social conversations. I have accepted that I often need more time for myself than many of my peers and that I may not always be able to participate in the same social activities as them.

My schizophrenia diagnosis, however, is much more of a challenge for me to identify with. I was diagnosed with schizophrenia later in life, when I was in my twenties. When I think about my schizophrenia, I do not feel like it is part of who I am. I struggle with my mental illness every day and I am constantly trying to cope with the symptoms, such as hallucinations and delusions, that come with it. It is difficult for me to accept these symptoms and to try to make sense of them.

I have found that the only way to reconcile my autism and schizophrenia diagnoses is to find an identity that incorporates both. I have come to the realization that I am both autistic and schizophrenic and that I can create an identity that incorporates both of my diagnoses. I have learned to accept my autistic traits and to embrace them as part of who I am. I have also learned to accept my schizophrenic symptoms and to work towards managing them.

I have also come to terms with the fact that I do not have to let my schizophrenia define who I am. I have come to the realization that my schizophrenia does not have to be my only identity. I can define myself based on my autistic traits and by the positive things I do in spite of the challenges I face. I can take pride in my talents and interests and focus on my strengths. I can define myself based on the things I do, not the things that I cannot do.

In the end, I have come to accept that my schizophrenia

diagnosis does not have to define my identity. I have found that I can find an identity that incorporates both my autism and schizophrenia diagnoses. I can proudly identify as both autistic and schizophrenic and work to create a positive identity based on the things I can do. I can embrace my autistic traits and my schizophrenic symptoms and create an identity that reflects who I am.

CHAPTER 7 MY EXPERIENCE WITH PSYCHIATRISTS

It feels like the fast food of mental health when I think about seeing a psychiatrist to treat my mental health. It's something I do out of necessity, yet I often feel like my time is wasted in the office of my psychiatrist. From the time I'm led in and sat down to when I'm told I no longer need to be there, the entire session usually lasts no more than five minutes. In that time, my psychiatrist prescribes me powerful medications, seemingly no matter what I've come in for. It often feels like he's not making any effort to get to know me as a person, nor to understand the root cause of my current mental health state.

This feeling of being misunderstood by my psychiatrist is a significant source of distress in itself. Thus, I've come up with a list of twenty key strategies to help me make the most of my time in the psychiatrist's office to ensure that my psychiatrist has a clear understanding of who I am and what I need.

Firstly, I make sure to come prepared. I write down my thoughts and feelings in advance, so that I'm able to articulate them to my psychiatrist. I also jot down any questions I may have for the psychiatrist, and I make sure to bring any medical records that may be relevant to the session.

I also make sure to come in with an open mind. I don't enter the session with any particular expectations, as I know that each appointment can be different. I remain open to my psychiatrist's advice, and I'm willing to try things that may be out of my comfort zone.

Additionally, I practice active listening. I pay close attention to what the psychiatrist is saying, and I ask questions if I don't understand something. I make sure to give my psychiatrist a chance to explain things in full before I interject.

When it comes to communicating my thoughts and feelings, I stay away from being too emotional. I try to remain calm and collected, as I want to ensure that I'm taken seriously. I also avoid being too vague, and instead provide clear details and examples to avoid confusion.

I also refrain from using jargon and medical terms. I avoid using words that may be too complicated or unfamiliar, as I want to make sure that my psychiatrist is able to understand me fully.

I also make sure to be honest with my psychiatrist. I don't hide any details, no matter how embarrassing or difficult they may be. I want my psychiatrist to have the full picture, so that I can receive the best treatment possible.

I also pay attention to body language. I make sure to sit up straight, maintain eye contact, and use my hands appropriately when I speak. I know that how I present myself and the way I carry myself can have an impact on the session.

I also make sure to ask my psychiatrist questions. I ask questions about my current mental health state, any medications I'm taking, and any treatments I may be considering. Asking questions helps to ensure that I'm informed about my mental health and any steps I can take to improve it.

I also practice self-reflection. I take time to think about my current mental health state and take stock of what has been working and what hasn't. This helps me to better communicate my progress (or lack thereof) to my psychiatrist.

I also make sure to be patient. I know that there are a lot of people who need to be seen, and I am willing to wait my turn. I also don't rush the psychiatrist, and instead give him time to think of the best course of action.

I also explain my feelings in terms of symptoms. For example, instead of telling my psychiatrist that I'm feeling "sad", I explain that I'm having trouble getting out of bed in the mornings, or that I'm having difficulty concentrating. This helps the psychiatrist to better understand the gravity of my mental health state.

I also make sure to bring someone with me when I visit the psychiatrist. Having a friend or family member with me in the session can help to provide a different perspective and can help to provide clarity on any points that may be confusing.

I also make sure to be mindful of time. I make sure to plan ahead, so that I don't run out of time during the session. I also stay on track and keep my questions to a minimum, so that I don't take too much of the psychiatrist's time.

Finally, I make sure to talk about what I'm doing to better my mental health. I tell my psychiatrist about any activities or things I'm doing to try and manage my mental health, like journaling or exercising. I also make sure to ask my psychiatrist for advice and resources that can help me continue to improve my mental health.

These twenty key strategies help me to make the most of my time in the psychiatrist's office. They help to ensure that my psychiatrist understands who I am and what I need. I've found that by remaining organized, open, honest, and articulate, I have better appointments with my psychiatrist. It may not be the most glamorous part of my mental health journey, but I'm grateful that I'm able to access a psychiatrist to help me with my mental health.

CHAPTER 8
EMPLOYMENT CHALLENGES WITH A DUAL DIAGNOSIS

Maintaining employment is a challenge for anybody, but for individuals diagnosed with both autism and schizophrenia, the task can be even more challenging. Both autism and schizophrenia can make it difficult to understand social cues, cope with stress, and interact in the workplace. This article will look at 25 ways in which autism makes employment difficult for the individual, 25 ways in which schizophrenia makes employment difficult for the individual, and 20 key strategies that a person can use to overcome dual diagnosis and maintain employment.

25 Ways Autism Makes Employment Difficult

1. Difficulty with Communication: Autism can affect an individual's ability to communicate their ideas and thoughts in a clear and concise manner, which can make it difficult to ask questions, give feedback, and interact with colleagues.

2. Difficulty Interpreting Social Cues: An individual with

autism may have difficulty interpreting social cues, which can make it difficult to interact and collaborate with coworkers.

3. Poor Social Skills: People with autism often struggle to make small talk and maintain relationships with coworkers, which can make it difficult to interact in the workplace.

4. Difficulty Following Directions: Individuals with autism may have difficulty following instructions, which can make it difficult to complete tasks on time and as directed.

5. Poor Executive Functioning: People with autism may struggle with executive functioning skills such as organization, time management, and planning, which can make it difficult to manage tasks and complete work on time.

6. Poor Problem Solving: Individuals with autism may struggle to come up with creative solutions to workplace issues, which can make it difficult to contribute meaningfully to the team.

7. Difficulty with Change: People with autism may have difficulty adjusting to changes in the workplace, which can make it difficult to stay on top of the latest trends and technologies.

8. Sensory Overload: People with autism can be easily overwhelmed by sensory input, which can make it difficult to focus in an office environment.

9. Anxiety: Individuals with autism may struggle with anxiety, which can make it difficult to complete tasks or interact with colleagues.

10. Difficulty Managing Stress: People with autism may have difficulty managing stress, which can make it difficult to stay productive in the workplace.

11. Difficulty with Prioritization: Individuals with autism may struggle to prioritize tasks, which can make it difficult to stay organized in the workplace.

12. Difficulty Understanding Nonverbal Communication: People with autism may struggle to understand nonverbal communication such as body language and facial expressions, which can make it difficult to understand conversations.

13. Poor Time Management: Individuals with autism may have difficulty managing their time, which can make it difficult to meet deadlines.

14. Difficulty Understanding Social Norms: People with autism may have difficulty understanding social norms, which can make it difficult to interact with colleagues and customers.

15. Poor Impulse Control: Individuals with autism may struggle with impulse control, which can make it difficult to maintain control in the workplace.

16. Poor Memory: People with autism may have difficulty remembering things, which can make it difficult to stay on top of tasks and projects.

17. Poor Self-Awareness: Individuals with autism may lack self-awareness, which can make it difficult to recognize and address their own strengths and weaknesses.

18. Hyper-Focusing: People with autism may be prone to

hyper-focusing, which can make it difficult to switch tasks and stay productive.

19. Difficulty Adapting to Change: Individuals with autism may have difficulty adapting to changes in the workplace, which can make it difficult to stay on top of tasks and projects.

20. Poor Self-Regulation: People with autism may have difficulty regulating their emotions, which can make it difficult to stay calm in stressful situations.

21. Difficulty with Social Situations: Individuals with autism may have difficulty understanding social situations, which can make it difficult to interact in the workplace.

22. Lack of Eye Contact: People with autism may lack eye contact, which can make it difficult to make a good first impression with colleagues.

23. Difficulty with Conversations: Individuals with autism may have difficulty carrying on a conversation, which can make it difficult to interact with colleagues and customers.

24. Difficulty Understanding Tone: People with autism may have difficulty understanding the tone of a conversation, which can make it difficult to interpret conversations in the workplace.

25. Difficulty with Multi-Tasking: Individuals with autism may have difficulty multi-tasking, which can make it difficult to stay on top of multiple tasks at once.

25 Ways Schizophrenia Makes Employment Difficult
1. Difficulty Concentrating: Schizophrenia can affect an individual's ability to concentrate, which can make it

difficult to stay on task and complete work.

2. Poor Executive Functioning: People with schizophrenia may struggle with executive functioning skills such as organization, time management, and planning, which can make it difficult to manage tasks and complete work on time.

3. Poor Social Skills: Individuals with schizophrenia often struggle to make small talk and maintain relationships with coworkers, which can make it difficult to interact in the workplace.

4. Difficulty Interpreting Social Cues: People with schizophrenia may have difficulty interpreting social cues, which can make it difficult to interact and collaborate with coworkers.

5. Difficulty Understanding Social Norms: Individuals with schizophrenia may have difficulty understanding social norms, which can make it difficult to interact with colleagues and customers.

6. Poor Memory: People with schizophrenia may have difficulty remembering things, which can make it difficult to stay on top of tasks and projects.

7. Poor Problem Solving: Individuals with schizophrenia may struggle to come up with creative solutions to workplace issues, which can make it difficult to contribute meaningfully to the team.

8. Difficulty Communicating: People with schizophrenia may have difficulty expressing their ideas and thoughts in a clear and concise manner, which can make it difficult to ask questions, give feedback, and interact with colleagues.

9. Poor Impulse Control: Individuals with schizophrenia may struggle with impulse control, which can make it difficult to maintain control in the workplace.

10. Difficulty Managing Stress: People with schizophrenia may have difficulty managing stress, which can make it difficult to stay productive in the workplace.

11. Poor Time Management: Individuals with schizophrenia may have difficulty managing their time, which can make it difficult to meet deadlines.

12. Hallucinations and Delusions: People with schizophrenia may experience hallucinations and delusions, which can make it difficult to focus on tasks and interact with colleagues.

13. Difficulty with Change: Individuals with schizophrenia may have difficulty adjusting to changes in the workplace, which can make it difficult to stay on top of the latest trends and technologies.

14. Anxiety: People with schizophrenia may struggle with anxiety, which can make it difficult to complete tasks or interact with colleagues.

15. Difficulty Adapting to Change: Individuals with schizophrenia may have difficulty adapting to changes in the workplace, which can make it difficult to stay on top of tasks and projects.

16. Poor Self-Awareness: People with schizophrenia may lack self-awareness, which can make it difficult to recognize and address their own strengths and weaknesses.

17. Difficulty with Prioritization: Individuals with schizophrenia may struggle to prioritize tasks, which can make it difficult to stay organized in the workplace.

18. Difficulty Understanding Tone: People with schizophrenia may have difficulty understanding the tone of a conversation, which can make it difficult to interpret conversations in the workplace.

19. Difficulty Understanding Nonverbal Communication: Individuals with schizophrenia may struggle to understand nonverbal communication such as body language and facial expressions, which can make it difficult to understand conversations.

20. Difficulty with Multi-Tasking: People with schizophrenia may have difficulty multi-tasking, which can make it difficult to stay on top of multiple tasks at once.

20 Key Strategies to Overcome Dual Diagnosis and Maintain Employment

1. Create a Support Network: Creating a strong support network of family, friends, and professionals can provide much-needed emotional and practical support when it comes to managing employment.

2. Find the Right Job: It is important to find a job that is suited to the individual's abilities and interests. This will ensure more job satisfaction and success.

3. Get Familiar with the Workplace: Becoming familiar with the workplace can help the individual to better understand the expectations and requirements of the job.

4. Ask Questions: Asking questions can help the individual to better understand the job and their role in the

workplace.

5. Take Care of Yourself: It is important to take care of one's physical, mental, and emotional health in order to maintain employment.

6. Stay Organized: Staying organized can help the individual to manage tasks and projects more effectively.

7. Set Goals: Setting goals can help the individual to stay motivated and focused on the tasks at hand.

8. Practice Mindfulness: Practicing mindfulness can help the individual to stay grounded and focused in the workplace.

9. Prepare for Interviews: Preparing for job interviews can help the individual to make a good first impression and get the job they want.

10. Develop a Schedule: Developing a routine and sticking to it can help the individual to better manage their time and stay on task.

11. Use Lists and Reminders: Making lists and using reminders can help the individual to better manage their tasks and stay organized.

12. Take Breaks: Taking regular breaks can help the individual to refresh and refocus in the workplace.

13. Manage Stress: It is important to find ways to manage stress in order to stay productive in the workplace.

14. Seek Accommodations: Seeking accommodations in the workplace can help the individual to better manage their work and stay on top of tasks.

15. Ask for Help: Asking for help is okay and can help the individual to stay on top of tasks.

16. Practice Self-Care: Practicing self-care can help the individual to stay grounded and manage their emotions in the workplace.

17. Find an Advocate: Finding an advocate in the workplace can help the individual to better manage their work and stay on top of tasks.

18. Set Boundaries: Setting boundaries can help the individual to better manage their work and stay on top of tasks.

19. Take Time for Yourself: Taking time for oneself can help the individual to stay grounded and focused in the workplace.

20. Seek Professional Help: Seeking professional help can help the individual to better manage their mental health and stay on top of tasks.

Finding and keeping a job can be challenging for individuals diagnosed with autism and schizophrenia. Both conditions can affect an individual's ability to communicate, interact, and stay organized in the workplace. By creating a strong support network, finding the right job, becoming familiar with the workplace, staying organized, and taking care of one's physical, mental, and emotional health, an individual with dual diagnosis can have success in employment. It is also important to ask for help and seek professional help to better manage mental health and stay on top of tasks. With the right strategies, an individual with dual diagnosis can overcome the challenges of employment and find success.

43

CHAPTER 9 FAMILY RELATIONSHIPS

Living with a dual diagnosis of autism and schizophrenia can be overwhelming and difficult to manage. For those with a dual diagnosis, life can be especially challenging because they must balance the difficulties of both conditions while navigating the social world. For individuals with a dual diagnosis, social relationships, especially with family, can be strained due to misunderstandings or lack of understanding of their mental illness. This can lead to tension, frustration, and even isolation. However, there are key strategies that individuals with a dual diagnosis can use to make and keep friends, despite the challenges their mental illness poses.

When it comes to family relationships, individuals with a dual diagnosis can feel especially misunderstood or even judged harshly by family, who may not understand the complexities of their condition. In this situation, it is important for the individual to explain the diagnosis in a way that family members will understand and to be patient with their reactions and responses. It is also important to ensure that the individual focuses on their strengths, rather than emphasizing their weaknesses. This can help maintain healthy family relationships and provide a safe space for the individual to express themselves and their feelings.

One of the biggest struggles individuals with a dual diagnosis face when it comes to social relationships is making and maintaining those relationships. It can be especially difficult to make new friends when one is experiencing psychosis. In these cases, it is important for the individual to be honest about their condition and to focus on positive activities or conversations. It can also be helpful to join a support group or attend social events to meet new people. Furthermore, if the individual is comfortable, they can discuss their diagnosis with friends, as this can help build understanding and empathy.

When it comes to social relationships, individuals with a dual diagnosis can also struggle to maintain them due to the symptoms of their mental illness. For example, paranoia can lead to distrust, withdrawal, and isolation. To combat this, it is important to communicate honestly and openly about the individual's condition and to practice self-care and stress management techniques. Additionally, it is important to be aware of triggers that may lead to psychosis or difficult emotions and to have a plan in place to manage them.

Despite the challenges posed by a dual diagnosis, individuals can use key strategies to make and keep friends. To start, it is important to identify what kind of relationships the individual wants and to set boundaries on what is acceptable and what is not. Additionally, it is important to focus on activities that bring joy and comfort, such as art or music, as this can help build trust and safety in relationships. Furthermore, individuals should take time to reflect on their own strengths and weaknesses, as this can help build self-confidence and allow them to better interact with others.

Another key strategy for individuals with a dual diagnosis is to practice active listening and communication. This involves actively listening to the other person without interruption and responding in an appropriate manner. Additionally, it is important to practice good self-care, such as getting adequate sleep, eating nutritious meals, and engaging in regular physical activity. This can help to manage stress and make it easier to interact with others.

Finally, it is important to be open and honest with friends. This means being honest about one's diagnosis and feelings, as this can help to build understanding and trust. It is also important to be aware of one's triggers and to have a plan in place to manage them, as this can help to prevent a relapse or psychosis. Additionally, it is important to recognize one's limits and to take time for self-care.

In summary, living with a dual diagnosis of autism and schizophrenia can be especially challenging when it comes to social relationships. Family relationships can be strained due to misunderstandings or lack of understanding of one's condition. Additionally, making and maintaining social relationships can be difficult due to the symptoms of one's mental illness. However, there are key strategies individuals with a dual diagnosis can use to make and keep friends, despite the challenges posed by their mental illness. These include identifying the kind of relationships one wants, practicing active listening and communication, and being open and honest about one's diagnosis and feelings. By implementing these strategies, individuals with a dual diagnosis can make and maintain meaningful relationships.

CHAPTER 10
CONCLUSION

The journey to overcoming the dual diagnosis of autism and schizophrenia was a complicated one and one that I am proud to say I have overcome. Over the past decade, I have used various strategies, perseverance, and the unwavering support of my family and friends to transform my life and make tremendous progress in achieving a fulfilling and meaningful life.

My story is one of hope and possibility; it serves as a reminder to everyone struggling with mental health challenges that recovery is possible. My story is also a testament to the power of determination, strength, and resilience. Through my struggles and successes, I have come to understand that my journey is truly remarkable and I am determined to share my story with others in the hopes of inspiring them to find the courage to keep going and never give up.

My journey has been an emotionally and mentally challenging one, but I am so thankful for the 25 key strategies I was able to use to overcome psychosis and live my best life. These strategies have not only helped me to cope with the chaos and difficulties that come with the dual diagnosis of autism and schizophrenia, but have also helped me to live a more peaceful, fulfilled life.

I am proud to say that I am thriving today. I am healthy and happy, and I am ready to take on any challenges that come my way. I am also excited for what my future holds and am eager to continue to share my story with those who may be struggling on a similar journey.

My journey of overcoming autism and schizophrenia has been a long and difficult one, but it has been worth each and every step. I am immensely grateful to all of my friends and family who have been by my side throughout this process and have provided me with the love and support that I needed to make it through.

This journey has been one of the greatest challenges I have ever faced, but I am so proud of the progress I have made. I am thankful for the strategies that I have used throughout this process and am confident that I will continue to use them to ensure that I am living my best life. I am also thankful to have the opportunity to share my story in the hopes of inspiring those who may be struggling in the same way.

My story of overcoming autism and schizophrenia is an incredible reminder that anything is possible, and I am so proud and thankful for the progress I have made over the past decade. From the bottom of my heart, I thank my family and friends for providing me with the love and support I needed to make it through, and for believing in me when I sometimes couldn't believe in myself.

I am proud to have made it through this journey and am confident that I will continue to live my best life from here on out.

ABOUT THE AUTHOR

Travis Breeding

Travis is the author of over 25 books on mental health and autism.   He loves to travel to share his story. Find out more about him at www.travisebreeding.com.

BOOKS BY THIS AUTHOR

I'm Not Unlikeable: I Just Operate On A Different Set Of Rules

Do you know someone living with autism who has struggled to find acceptance and understanding? If so, I'm Not Unlikeable, I Just Operate on a Different Set of Rules may be the book for them. This intriguing autobiography by Travis Breeding is about one autistic adult's life journey, from being undiagnosed until age 22, to then discovering the underlying cause behind his relational and social struggles—autism!

Travis Breeding dives deep into his extraordinary story —one filled with immense personal transformation. He reveals how his journey led him to come to terms with multiple comorbid conditions, such as anxiety, depression, misdiagnosis of schizoaffective disorder in 2013 at age 28 and inappropriate social boundaries making it challenging to effectively manage communication and relationships.

Through adversity and hope comes great recovery – this book tells the passionate story that leads up to Travis' goal of applying Behavior Analysis techniques to help others have more meaningful lives. A highly recommended read for anyone who wants to explore what it's like for an autistic adult navigating through uncertain times and gaining new insight into living their best life possible!

Breaking The Mold: Empowering Autistic Adults In The Workplace

Breaking the Mold" explores the unique challenges and strengths of autistic adults in the workplace. Through a collection of personal stories and expert insights, this book sheds light on the obstacles faced by the autistic community and provides practical strategies for empowering individuals on the spectrum to reach their full potential in their careers. This empowering guide is a must-read for anyone looking to promote diversity, inclusiveness, and understanding in the workplace. Whether you are an autistic adult seeking guidance, an ally looking to support the community, or an HR professional striving to create a more neurodiverse workplace, this book will provide valuable insights and inspiration to help you break the mold and unleash the full potential of autistic adults in the workplace.

Practical Solution For Practical Problems: An Autistic View Of Applied Behavior Analysis

Applied behavior analysis is a field of psychology that deals with the modification of behavior. It is one of the few interventions that has been shown to be effective with individuals on the autism spectrum. This book is geared towards practitioners who wish to learn more about the advanced topics related to applied behavior analysis. It discusses social validity, medical necessity, pragmatic language, generalization and application of social skills, and dosage amounts of applied behavior analysis to be provided to individuals with autism spectrum disorder.

Nature Vs. Nurture In Aba: The Tale Of Discrete Trial Training And Natural Envionrment Teaching

"Nature vs. Nurture in ABA: The Tale of Discrete Trial Training and Natural Environment Teaching" is a comprehensive exploration of the ongoing debate within the field of Applied Behavior Analysis (ABA) regarding the most effective methods of teaching and behavior modification. This book delves into the contrasting approaches of discrete trial training and natural environment teaching, examining their respective strengths and limitations. Through a careful analysis of current research and practical case studies, the book provides insight into the role of both nature and nurture in shaping behavior and offers guidance for practitioners seeking to incorporate evidence-based practices into their work. Whether you are a seasoned ABA professional or a student just entering the field, this book is a must-read for anyone interested in the latest developments in ABA and the ongoing nature vs. nurture debate.

Overwhelming Emotions: Navigating The Sensory Storm Of Autism

Are you or someone you love struggling with overwhelming emotions on the autism spectrum? Look no further! 'Overwhelming Emotions: Navigating the Sensory Storm of Autism' provides a comprehensive guide to managing emotions and sensory experiences in autism.

With a focus on practical techniques and strategies, this book covers topics such as regulating emotions, coping with sensory overload, and building resilience. Through a combination of expert advice, personal stories, and interactive exercises, you'll gain a deeper understanding of the unique challenges faced by individuals on the spectrum and learn how to navigate the sensory storm with ease. Whether you're a parent, caregiver, or someone on the spectrum, 'Overwhelming Emotions' is the ultimate tool for managing emotions and sensory experiences.